HOW TO WRITE A SONG ON THE GUITAR

BY ALLISON JAMES

ISBN 978-1-70513-704-8

Exclusively Distributed By

WILLIS MUSIC

HAL•LEONARD®

Visit Hal Leonard Online at
www.halleonard.com

Contact us:
Hal Leonard
7777 West Bluemound Road
Milwaukee, WI 53213
Email: info@halleonard.com

In Europe, contact:
Hal Leonard Europe Limited
42 Wigmore Street
Marylebone, London, W1U 2RN
Email: info@halleonardeurope.com

In Australia, contact:
Hal Leonard Australia Pty. Ltd.
4 Lentara Court
Cheltenham, Victoria, 3192 Australia
Email: info@halleonard.com.au

A NOTE TO THE TEACHER

From me to you, teacher to teacher, thank you for choosing this workbook to aid in the musical growth of your student.

This workbook was designed for the beginning songwriter and budding artist, creating a safe space to express themselves through music.

In my experience, it can be an uncomfortable process for some students to be vulnerable enough to open up to their own creativity. My hope is that you, as a teacher and guide, can maintain that safe space for them to create freely. It is especially important to not judge or criticize their inner artist. Let them explore freely; let their ear guide them. Let them find their own chords, melody, lyrics, and story they want to tell. The more you allow their inner artist to guide them in the beginning, the more they will be able to create openly and freely, without feeling stifled. When that is achieved, it will be easier to add in traditional theory techniques as needed. A delicate balance between creativity and theory will need to be maintained. This workbook is designed to help you with this, each step of the way. Be gentle, be supportive, and the results will be amazing!

Allison James
www.songwritingworkbooks.com

TABLE OF CONTENTS

INTRODUCTION: A Note to the Songwriter

Welcome! You are about to write your first song!

The materials needed are:

- Pen or pencil

- Guitar

- Creativity

- Audio recording device (optional)

This workbook will guide you through the process of writing a complete song with **chords**, **melody**, and **lyrics**, using a guitar.

You will:

- choose **CHORDS** you like

- add a **MELODY** to those chords

- add **LYRICS** to the melody

- **NOTATE** your melody and complete a chord chart.

NOTE:
Be sure to begin with a properly TUNED guitar. If you need help, there are many resources available online, as well as helpful apps in the App Store.

Songs can be written in many different keys. A **key** is the tonal center of a song. Your song will be in the key of **C Major**. It is the easiest key to begin with because the key of C Major contains no sharps or flats.

Here is the notated C Major scale:

Here it is on a keyboard:

Here it is on a guitar:

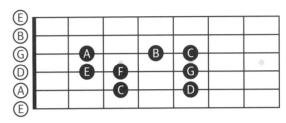

(Note: This scale on the guitar is an octave lower than what is written on the staff intentionally, to give you the easiest position to play it.)

Your song will also be in a basic time signature:

This means the song will be counted in sections of 4 beats. This will be explained in more detail later on.

You will write one chorus and two verses arranged in the following order (the chorus is repeated):

Verse 1 - CHORUS - Verse 2 – CHORUS

This song structure can also be referred to as **A - B - A - B** (ABAB) form.

Because the chorus is repeated, it will have the same melody and lyrics. The two verses will have the *same* melody but *different* lyrics.

This workbook is designed so that you will be able to step away whenever needed, then come back and pick up where you left off. (Some may be able to finish it in one session!)

**Turn the page
when you are ready to start.**

CHAPTER 1
Chords

CHORDS are a group of 3 or more notes played together.

1A. Learn the chords in the key of C Major.

Below are the chords in the key of C Major. The chords are built on top of each note in the C Major scale.

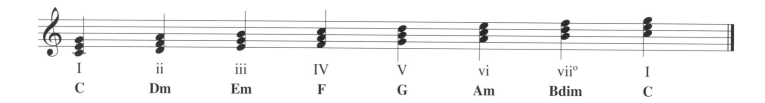

Each chord is labeled with a Roman numeral and a letter name.

Chords are labeled according to their letter name by the key you play in.

All chords in all keys can be labeled with Roman numerals:

- Uppercase Roman numerals (I, IV, and V) signify **major** chords.

- Lowercase Roman numerals (ii, iii, vi) signify **minor** chords.

- Lowercase Roman numeral with a circle (vii°) signifies a **diminished** chord.

Here are those same chords on the guitar:

C Major (I)
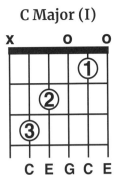
X   O   O
① ② ③
C E G C E

D minor (ii)
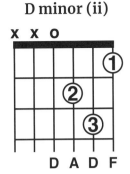
X X O
① ② ③
D A D F

E minor (iii)
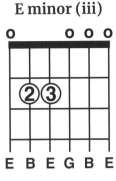
O   O O O
② ③
E B E G B E

F Major (IV)
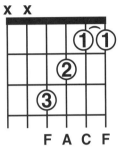
X X
① ① ② ③
F A C F

G Major (V)
O O O
② ③ ④
G B D G B G

A minor (vi)
X O   O
① ② ③
A E A C F

B diminished (vii°)
X X X
① ② ③
B D F

KEY:
- 1–4: the finger to use on that string.
- X: don't strum that string.
- O: an open string. Strum that string with the rest of them, even if there is not a finger on it.
- The letters below are the notes being played.

C Major
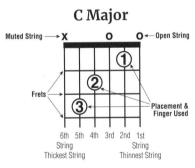

Muted String → X   O   O ← Open String

Frets →

① ② ③

Placement & Finger Used

6th 5th 4th 3rd 2nd 1st
String   String
Thickest String   Thinnest String

Full chord versions:
For most beginners these full chords are quite difficult. We've used the simplified versions of F and B above, but here are the full chords if you want to give them a try!

F Major
① ① ① ② ③ ④
F C F A C F

B diminished
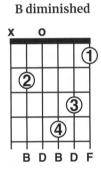
X O
① ② ③ ④
B D B D F

(Note: These chords are the same as the ones on the staff on page 6, but they are not necessarily in the same inversion or place on the staff. We've done this intentionally, to make it easier for the new guitar player.)

Your Turn

Left Handed   Right Handed

Play each of these chords with your guitar. Place your fingers on the strings with your fret hand. With your other hand strum the strings just once per chord, for now. Use the simplified chords as needed.

Practice all of them until they are easy to play.

1B. Choose 4 chords for your song.

Play around with the chords you have just learned in C Major.

Play them in several different orders, mixing and matching. Do this until you find 4 chords that you think sound good when played one after the other.

You are creating a **chord progression**. A chord progression is a sequence of chords played one after the other, and then repeated.

Here is a common chord progression in C Major. Practice playing it:

C Major   F Major   G Major   C Major

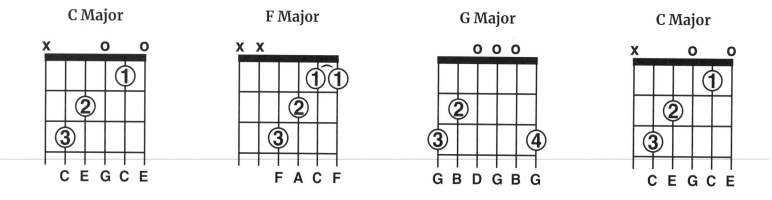

C Major   F Major   G Major   C Major

C E G C E   F A C F   G B D G B G   C E G C E

Here are other common chord progressions in the key of C Major:

F – G – F – C

Am – Em – F – C

C – Am – Dm – G

Am – F – G – C

Your Turn

Write your chosen chords below:

_____ _____ _____ _____

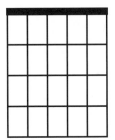 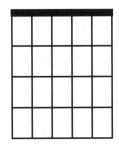 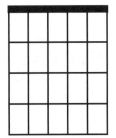 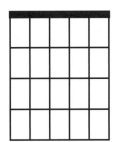

Write out the notes of your chords on these blank fretboards.

Now play the 4 chords slowly, in the order written.
Repeat until you feel comfortable switching from one chord to the next.

1C. Simplify the chords.

On the next few pages you will begin to form a chord chart.

A **chord chart** organizes chords of a song alongside a time signature.

The chords in these charts are simplified and written in a shorthand notation so they can be read quickly.

MAJOR chords are written with just their letter because the "major" part is implied. For example:

C Major = C

MINOR chords are written as their letter followed by a lowercase "m" to inform the performer that it is a minor chord. For example:

D minor = Dm

DIMINISHED chords can be written as their letter followed by "dim" to inform the reader it is a diminished chord.

B diminished = Bdim

You will become more and more comfortable reading the shorthand chords and finding different patterns to play. Practice and experiment.

Here again are the chords we've been using thus far:

C Major – F Major – G Major – C Major

These chords would be simplified like this:

C – F – G – C

Your Turn

Write the simplified (shorthand) notation of the chords you chose:

_____   _____   _____   _____

Practice playing the chords by reading *only* the shorthand notation.
It is important to feel very comfortable with this, because this is what you
will be doing in your final chord chart.

1D. Add rhythm.

Rhythm is the measured arrangement and flow of music.

In pop or jazz, drums usually play the rhythm sections of songs, but for now it has to be all you!

As mentioned in the Introduction, you will use a simple $\frac{4}{4}$ time signature. To do this, start by counting to 4 EVENLY, and then repeat. Each repetition of 1-4 is called a **measure**.

Your Turn

Count out loud EVENLY: **1 2 3 4 | 1 2 3 4 | 1 2 3 4 | 1 2 3 4**

This is how a $\frac{4}{4}$ time signature is counted.

1E. Put the chords in a $\frac{4}{4}$ time signature.

On the next page, place your chords in a small chord chart with a $\frac{4}{4}$ time signature.

With your guitar, play each chord 4 times. Hold the chord on the frets and strum down 4 times.

Once again, as practice, use the same C-F-G-C chords arranged in this small chord chart. The down arrow means to strum down towards the floor. Play each chord 4 times:

Chord:	$\frac{4}{4}$ | C C C C | F F F F | G G G G | C C C C |
Strum:	$\frac{4}{4}$ | ↓ ↓ ↓ ↓ | ↓ ↓ ↓ ↓ | ↓ ↓ ↓ ↓ | ↓ ↓ ↓ ↓ |
Counts:	| 1 2 3 4 | 1 2 3 4 | 1 2 3 4 | 1 2 3 4 |

Your Turn

Write your chord progression using the simplified chord notation in $\frac{4}{4}$ time.

Chord: ___ ___ ___ ___ | ___ ___ ___ ___ | ___ ___ ___ ___ | ___ ___ ___ ___

1ST CHORD   **2ND CHORD**   **3RD CHORD**   **4TH CHORD**

Strum: ↓ ↓ ↓ ↓ , ↓ ↓ ↓ ↓ , ↓ ↓ ↓ ↓ , ↓ ↓ ↓ ↓

Play the chord progression in $\frac{4}{4}$ time, then repeat.
Play until you can easily move from chord to chord.

Let's practice a couple other strumming patterns. Try strumming the first count, then letting the sound ring out for the next 3 counts.

Chord: ___ — — — | ___ — — — | ___ — — — | ___ — — —

Strum: ↓ — — — | ↓ — — — | ↓ — — — | ↓ — — —

Here's another easy strumming pattern:

Chord: ___ — ___ — | ___ — ___ — | ___ — ___ — | ___ — ___ —

Strum: ↓ — ↓ — | ↓ — ↓ — | ↓ — ↓ — | ↓ — ↓ —

It is up to you to decide how to play the rhythm of your chords.
These are just some options to start with.

Stay in the $\frac{4}{4}$ time signature and keep experimenting to see what you like best!

1F. Create a complete section.

You will now create a 16-measure section of your chords. Remember that one measure equals one set of counting to 4.

For this 16-measure section, you will repeat your 4-chord progression 4 times.

One entire section will make one verse. Repeat it to make your chorus, then again for your second verse, then again for your last chorus. More on this later.

For example, let's stay with the same chord progression: C, F, G, C. The dashes after each chord signify that the same chord is used for the whole measure with the strumming pattern you've chosen.

1.   **2.**

$\frac{4}{4}$ | C - - - | F - - - | G - - - | C - - - | C - - - | F - - - | G - - - | C - - - |

3.   **4.**

| C - - - | F - - - | G - - - | C - - - | C - - - | F - - - | G - - - | C - - - |

Your Turn

Write your chord progression here, completing one section.

1.   **2.**

$\frac{4}{4}$ | _ - - - | _ - - - | _ - - - | _ - - - | _ - - - | _ - - - | _ - - - | _ - - - |

3.   **4.**

| _ - - - | _ - - - | _ - - - | _ - - - | _ - - - | _ - - - | _ - - - | _ - - - |

Now play the chord progression for the entire section. You have now created a 16-measure section.

Play and practice this chord progression until it feels comfortable to play.

Additional Chord Options

If you have some music theory knowledge and find yourself wanting to add more texture to your song, experiment with these more advanced options. Otherwise, continue to Chapter 2.

1. **7th Chords.** These chords are a normal major or minor chord with a minor 7th note added. Look at the example below. For the G7 chord, the three notes of a normal G Major chord are played with a note added: the minor 7th above G, the note F. As you play the example, you will hear that the G7 (or V7 - remember Roman numerals?) resolves nicely into the C (I).

Using the chord progression of C – F – G – C:

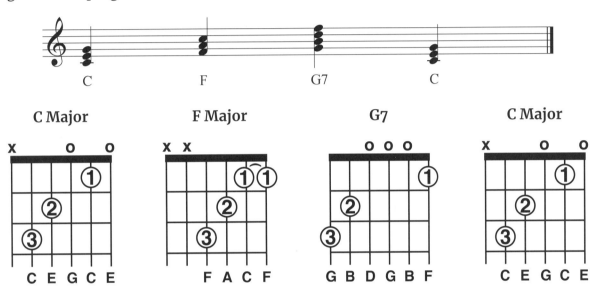

2. **Maj7 Chords:** These chords are a normal major chord with a major 7th note added. See the example below. For the Gmaj7 chord, the three normal notes of the G Major chord are played, with a note added: the major 7th above G, the note F♯. The maj7 chords have a more jazz/R&B sound to them. They also resolve nicely to C.

Using the chord progression of C – F – G – C:

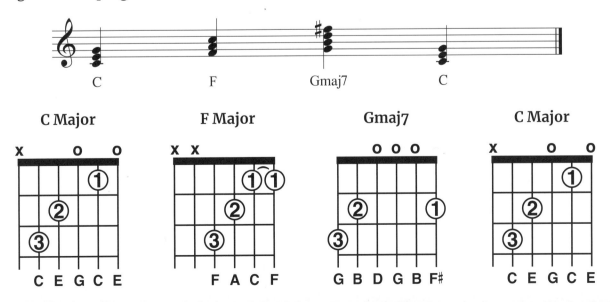

Additional Strumming Options

If you find yourself wanting to add more excitement to your rhythm, here are a few other strumming options. You may even want to choose one rhythm for your verses and a different one for your choruses. Practice them with your own chord progression or with our example chords.

C Major   F Major   G Major   C Major

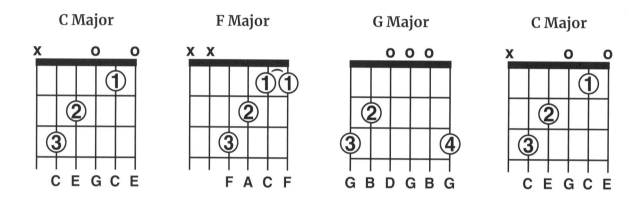

C Major   F Major   G Major   C Major

↓ = strum down towards the floor

↑ = strum up towards the sky

1.
```
|↓↑↓↑↓↑↓↑|↓↑↓↑↓ ↑↓↑|↓↑↓↑↓↑↓↑|↓↑↓↑↓↑↓↑|
|1 + 2 + 3 + 4 +|1 + 2 + 3 + 4 +|1 + 2 + 3 + 4 +|1 + 2 + 3 + 4 +|
```

2.
```
|↓  ↓  ↓  ↓↑|↓  ↓  ↓  ↓↑|↓  ↓  ↓  ↓↑|↓  ↓  ↓  ↓↑|
|1 + 2 + 3 + 4 +|1 + 2 + 3 + 4 +|1 + 2 + 3 + 4 +|1 + 2 + 3 + 4 +|
```

3.
```
|↓  ↓↑↓  ↓↑|↓  ↓↑↓  ↓↑|↓  ↓↑↓  ↓↑|↓  ↓↑↓  ↓↑|
|1 + 2 + 3 + 4 +|1 + 2 + 3 + 4 +|1 + 2 + 3 + 4 +|1 + 2 + 3 + 4 +|
```

CHAPTER 2
Melody

A **melody** is a sequence of single notes that you can put lyrics to.

For this song you will be creating 2 melodies:

1 melody for your verses (A sections) and

1 melody for your chorus (B section).

You will complete your ABAB song form:

A   B   A   B

(Verse 1)   (Chorus)   (Verse 2)   (Chorus)

Your Turn

Play the traditional nursery rhyme "Twinkle, Twinkle, Little Star"
on the next page.

First, play its chord progression (like you played yours).

Then, hum or sing the melody to "Twinkle, Twinkle."

When you are ready, play the chords AND sing the words.

Twinkle, Twinkle, Little Star

$\frac{4}{4}$ | C C C C | F F C C | F F C C | G G C C |

Lyrics: Twin-kle, twin-kle,   lit - tle   star,____   How I   won-der   what you are.____

Here are the chords C, F, and G if you need a reminder:

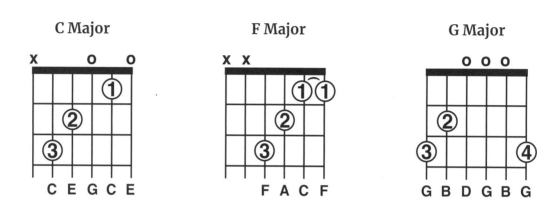

Playing these chords while humming or singing the melody is what you will be doing with your chord progression!

NOTE:
If you prefer to write your lyrics first, skip to Chapter 3 (Lyrics) on page 24, and then return to this chapter.

2A. Create the melody for the VERSE or A Section.

Create a melody for your verse!

On page 14, you finished one entire section of chords.

Now, create a melody to that 16-measure section. Call it the Verse or A Section.

Verse section melodies typically use lower notes than choruses. The melodies may even repeat.

Like "Twinkle, Twinkle, Little Star," hum a melody to your chords.

The easiest way to come up with a melody is to just start humming while you play your chords. Hum any note and go from there.

With trial and error, you will eventually find a sequence of notes that will sound great over your chords.

It is now your turn.
You can do it!

Your Turn

Create the melody for the VERSE (A Section) of your song.

Rewrite the chords here so you can look at them while you play:

VERSE (A Section)

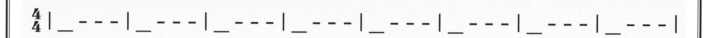

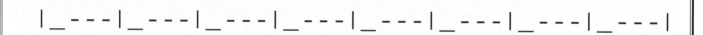

Play the chord progression in the 16-measure chart above,
using your chosen strumming style.

Hum while playing (or use *la-la-la* or another vowel sound you like).
Hum notes that sound good to you, in sentence-style phrases,
until you find something you like that sticks.

RECOMMENDED:
Record your melody on your phone or on another recording device.

2B. Create the melody for the CHORUS or B Section.

Create a melody for your chorus!

Chorus melodies are usually more complex and consist of higher notes because this is where the song begins to build. The chorus is the main idea of a song, in melody and lyrics.

Your Turn

Create the melody for the CHORUS (B Section) of your song.

Play your chord progression again.
This time, hum a different melody.

This melody is a *continuation* of your first one.
The melody for the VERSE (A) will lead right into the CHORUS (B).

Write your chords here and create your chorus melody:

CHORUS (B Section)

$\frac{4}{4}$ | _ - - - | _ - - - | _ - - - | _ - - - | _ - - - | _ - - - | _ - - - | _ - - - |

| _ - - - | _ - - - | _ - - - | _ - - - | _ - - - | _ - - - | _ - - - | _ - - - |

RECOMMENDED:
Record this on your recording device.

2C. Play the chords while humming your melodies.

The A Section melody will be sung in both VERSES.
The B Section melody will be sung in both CHORUSES.

Your Turn

Fill in the chords and play your entire song on the guitar
as you hum your newly written melodies!

VERSE 1 (A Section)

$\frac{4}{4}$ | _ - - - | _ - - - | _ - - - | _ - - - | _ - - - | _ - - - | _ - - - | _ - - - |

| _ - - - | _ - - - | _ - - - | _ - - - | _ - - - | _ - - - | _ - - - | _ - - - |

CHORUS (B Section)

| _ - - - | _ - - - | _ - - - | _ - - - | _ - - - | _ - - - | _ - - - | _ - - - |

| _ - - - | _ - - - | _ - - - | _ - - - | _ - - - | _ - - - | _ - - - | _ - - - |

VERSE 2 (A Section)

| _ - - - | _ - - - | _ - - - | _ - - - | _ - - - | _ - - - | _ - - - | _ - - - |

| _ - - - | _ - - - | _ - - - | _ - - - | _ - - - | _ - - - | _ - - - | _ - - - |

CHORUS (B Section)

| _ - - - | _ - - - | _ - - - | _ - - - | _ - - - | _ - - - | _ - - - | _ - - - |

| _ - - - | _ - - - | _ - - - | _ - - - | _ - - - | _ - - - | _ - - - | _ - - - |

Advanced Melody Options

The best way to learn to create good melodies is to analyze the melodies of existing songs that YOU love. What are some of them?

As you listen to them again, ask yourself:

1. Which lines of the verse melody repeat?
   - Are there 2 lines of repeating melody before it changes?
   - Are there 4 lines of repeating melody?
   - What is the same? What is different?

2. How does the melody of the verse differ from the melody of the chorus?
   - Does the verse use lower notes than the chorus?
   - Are any of the notes from the verses similar to the chorus?

3. What changes in the melody create a change in feeling?
   - Do lower notes make you feel different than higher notes?
   - What do higher notes make you feel?

4. What note does the song start on?
   - How does that correspond to the first chord and key of the song?

5. What note does the song end on?
   - How does that correspond to the last chord and key of the song?

Some popular practices used by professionals:

1. **The melody of the verse usually consists of lower notes than the melody in the chorus.** This is usually done to achieve a build-up in the chorus. Higher notes often signify an increase in energy and emotion.

2. **The song ends on the *tonic*.** This means that the last note of the song is usually the same as the first note of the key. For example, if the song is in the key of C, the last melody note is usually a C. This creates a resolution that feels natural to our ears.

3. **There is some form of repetition.** The melody lines in most modern pop songs will repeat in some way. Sometimes it is the first two lines that are the same melodically; often the second two also match. Sometimes the first four lines of the verse use the exact same melody. Repetition creates memorability. Most songwriters want to write catchy songs that people will remember.

CHAPTER 3
Lyrics

Lyrics are the words to a melody.

For this song you will be writing lyrics for
two verses and **one chorus**
in the A–B–A–B form.

You will only need to write one set of lyrics for the chorus
because the *same* lyrics will be sung in both.

Like this:

A	**B**	**A**	**B**
(Verse 1 Lyrics)	(Chorus Lyrics)	(Verse 2 Lyrics)	(Chorus Lyrics)

As an example, let's check out a familiar song on the next page.

This Old Man

Traditional Nursery Rhyme

A
Verse 1

This old man, he played one,
He played knick-knack on his thumb,

B
CHORUS

With a knick-knack paddy-whack, give the dog a bone,
This old man came rolling home.

A
Verse 2

This old man, he played two,
He played knick-knack on his shoe,

B
CHORUS

With a knick-knack paddy-whack, give the dog a bone,
This old man came rolling home.

Your Turn

Sing "This Old Man."

Notice that the Verse melodies are the same, but the lyrics are different.
Notice that the Chorus melodies are the same, and the lyrics are the same.

This is similar to what you will write for your song!

Writing the Chorus

3A. Write the lyrics for the Chorus.

Write the words to your song!

Now that you have created your melody,
start to think about *how* your melody sounds.

Does it sound sad? Is it happy?

This will give you a starting place with your lyrics and
what your song is going to be about.

It is usually easier to start with writing the chorus. Your chorus should contain the main theme
of your song. It will give you the foundation for what the rest of your song will be about.

While choruses give the main idea of a song, the verses supplement the chorus
by adding more detail to the story.

Your Turn

Your mission is simple: Free write.

On the next page, think of the melody you have created and write down EVERYTHING that
comes to mind. Leave the analyzing for later, just write!

3B. Narrow your ideas.

Read through what you have written and decide which lines and ideas you like best. Circle the parts that could be interesting lines or topics in your song.

Do you have a main idea or "hook"?

A *hook* is the line of the song that everyone will remember. It usually ends up being the song title.

What is the main theme of your song?
What emotion do you want to convey to the listener?

What story do you want to tell?

3C. Start forming your *chorus*.

On the next page, fill in your chords and start to write the lyrics to go with your B section. These will become the lyrics that will be sung to your melody.

Sing the lyrics to your melody over and over until you find the right words that fit. This step sometimes takes a bit of time. That's okay! Make it singable. Make it memorable. Make it yours.

Your Turn

Fill in your chords and lyrics.

CHORUS (B Section)

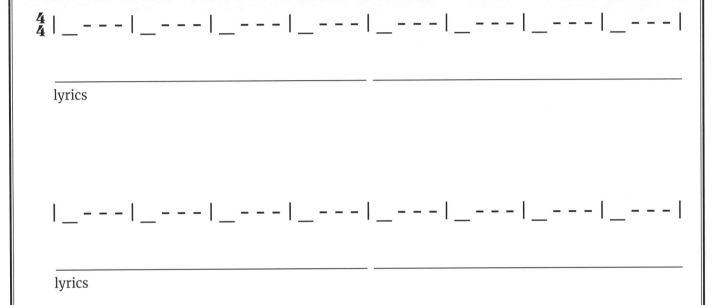

lyrics

lyrics

Play your chords in your chord chart above.
Then, play and sing your melody along with the new lyrics.

Writing the Verses

3D. For the verses, repeat the same process.

Verses tell the story to your song. They complement the chorus and should not compete with it musically.

Your Turn

Free write. Write freely.

Write down what comes to mind when you think of the melody
you have created for the verses.

Again, leave the analyzing for later—just write.

_____

_____

_____

_____

_____

_____

_____

_____

_____

_____

_____

_____

_____

_____

_____

_____

3E. Narrow your ideas.

Read through what you have written.
Then, decide which lines and ideas you like best.
Circle the parts you think could be the most interesting lines.

What will add to the story of your chorus?

Your Turn

(Circle) or underline the parts you like for your verse.

3F. Form your verses.

On the next page, fill in the chords.
Then, start to write the lyrics to go with the A section.

Repeat for each verse.

Your Turn

Fill in the chords and lyrics to your song.

Add the B section (Chorus) you already wrote.
This will help to ensure a flow to your song and your story.

VERSE 1 (A Section):

$\frac{4}{4}$ | _ - - - | _ - - - | _ - - - | _ - - - | _ - - - | _ - - - | _ - - - | _ - - - |

_____   _____
lyrics

| _ - - - | _ - - - | _ - - - | _ - - - | _ - - - | _ - - - | _ - - - | _ - - - |

_____   _____
lyrics

CHORUS (B Section):

| _ - - - | _ - - - | _ - - - | _ - - - | _ - - - | _ - - - | _ - - - | _ - - - |

_____   _____
lyrics

| _ - - - | _ - - - | _ - - - | _ - - - | _ - - - | _ - - - | _ - - - | _ - - - |

_____   _____
lyrics

VERSE 2 (A Section):

| _ - - - | _ - - - | _ - - - | _ - - - | _ - - - | _ - - - | _ - - - | _ - - - |

_____   _____
lyrics

| _ - - - | _ - - - | _ - - - | _ - - - | _ - - - | _ - - - | _ - - - | _ - - - |

_____   _____
lyrics

ADVANCED LYRIC OPTIONS

Like with melodies, one of the best ways to learn how to write lyrics is to **analyze** the lyrics of existing songs that you love. Name three of your favorite songs:

_____   _____   _____

Listen to these songs and ask yourself these questions (feel free to jot down answers and ideas):

1. What is the overall story of the song?

2. What phrase of the song is the "hook"?

    How does it relate to the story of the song?

    What makes it special or unique?

3. How do the verses add to the story?

    Do they add additional information to the story?

    Or do they just tell more of the same story?

4. What are the rhythms of the lyrics?

    Are the lyrics in any sort of pattern(s)?

    Which parts are more structured, and which parts are more flowing?

5. How do the rhythms of the lyrics change from the verse to the chorus?

Popular practices used by professional songwriters:

1. **Lyrics have syllabic patterns.**
   Popular songs have patterns in their lyrics, especially if the melody is the same in two lines or more. If you have a song that has the same melody in the first two lines, each line will often also have the same amount of syllables. The patterns are different from song to song, but the more songs you analyze, the more you will see that those patterns are there.

For example, here is a breakdown of the lyrics in "This Old Man":

This old man, he played one,
(3 syllables, 3 syllables,
creates repetition and balance)

He played knick-knack on his thumb,
(7 syllables, same as last line)

With a knick-knack paddy-whack, give the dog a bone,
(a break from patterns to create interest)

This old man came rolling home.
(7 syllables)

2. **There is a catchy hook.**
   Listen to almost any song on the radio and it will have a hook. The line with the hook in it is usually placed at the end of the chorus or even the end of the song. The hook can be the moral to the story or the catchiest part of the melody. It is often the title of the song.

3. **Lyrics rhyme, but are not *too* "rhyme-y."**
   A lot of popular songs have lyrics that rhyme, but when rhyming is mixed with predictability, your song can end up sounding cheesy. Most professional songwriters avoid this. When you are trying to rhyme, pick the most unpredictable rhyme that still makes sense to your story. Unexpected twists in your lyrics make your song even more interesting to your listener.

CHAPTER 4
Putting It All Together

It's finally time to put it all together.

4A. Fill out the chord chart on the next page, and play your complete song.

Your Turn

Fill in your chords and lyrics for your entire song.

Add the chords for all sections.

Add the lyrics for all sections.

Play and sing your completed song—
chords, melody, and lyrics all together!

Song Title: _____

Music & Lyrics by: _____

Verse 1

$\frac{4}{4}$ | _ - - - | _ - - - | _ - - - | _ - - - | _ - - - | _ - - - | _ - - - | _ - - - |

_____ _____
lyrics

| _ - - - | _ - - - | _ - - - | _ - - - | _ - - - | _ - - - | _ - - - | _ - - - |

_____ _____
lyrics

CHORUS

| _ - - - | _ - - - | _ - - - | _ - - - | _ - - - | _ - - - | _ - - - | _ - - - |

_____ _____
lyrics

| _ - - - | _ - - - | _ - - - | _ - - - | _ - - - | _ - - - | _ - - - | _ - - - |

_____ _____
lyrics

Verse 2

| _ - - - | _ - - - | _ - - - | _ - - - | _ - - - | _ - - - | _ - - - | _ - - - |

_____ _____
lyrics

| _ - - - | _ - - - | _ - - - | _ - - - | _ - - - | _ - - - | _ - - - | _ - - - |

_____ _____
lyrics

CHORUS

| _ - - - | _ - - - | _ - - - | _ - - - | _ - - - | _ - - - | _ - - - | _ - - - |

_____ _____
lyrics

| _ - - - | _ - - - | _ - - - | _ - - - | _ - - - | _ - - - | _ - - - | _ - - - |

_____ _____
lyrics

4B. Rewrite and make adjustments as needed.

Songs get written and rewritten, edited and reedited in the songwriting process.

It is normal to do that to yours too. Rewrite parts until you are happy with it.

Sometimes it is best to leave it for a day or two before coming back to it. With fresh ears and eyes, you will have a new perspective. New ideas might come to you in the shower, on the bus, on a walk, etc. Let it rest and return refreshed.

Things to consider to make your song the best it can be:

- Does it flow?
- Will your listener be able to relate?
- Do the lyrics from one section to another relate to the same ideas?
- Does your song have an overall message?
- Is the melody singable and can someone sing along?
- Do you like it?
- Is it catchy?
- Does it make you feel something?

Your Turn

Edit and rewrite as needed.

_____
_____
_____
_____
_____
_____
_____
_____
_____
_____
_____

We are almost there. Just one more step.

4C. Give your song a title.

Last, but definitely not least, your song needs a title!

Think about the main theme of your song and try to put it into a few words:

_____

_____

_____

Your Turn

Write the title at the top of your chord chart and voilà,
you have now completed your first song!

Be sure to add your name on the line: *Music & Lyrics by...*

You have completed your first song. Great job!

Now start writing your next one!

...that is, unless you'd like to learn to NOTATE your song.

If so, turn the page!

CHAPTER 5
Notation (Optional)

This chapter is for songwriters who want to learn the tradition of writing their songs on a musical staff.

Musical notation is writing notes down on a music staff. Here, again, are some notes on a treble staff:

C   D   E   F   G   A   B   C   D   E   F   G

Here are those notes on the guitar:

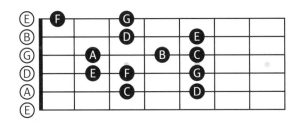

(As mentioned before, these notes are intentionally an octave lower than shown on the staff, for simplification.)

Another way to write a chord chart (or lead sheet) is to notate your melody on a treble staff. Your chords will be written above each measure and your lyrics below each measure.

Here is the original example of "Twinkle, Twinkle, Little Star":

$\frac{4}{4}$ | C C C C | F F C C | F F C C | G G C C |

Lyrics: Twin-kle, twin-kle,   lit - tle   star, ____   How I   won-der   what you   are. ____

The notated version is on the next page. The melody is written out so that you know what to sing, and the chords are above the staff so that you know what to play.

Your Turn

To begin to understand how to notate your melody, play the melody line of
"Twinkle, Twinkle, Little Star" on your guitar.
Use the fretboard on the opposite page for reference.

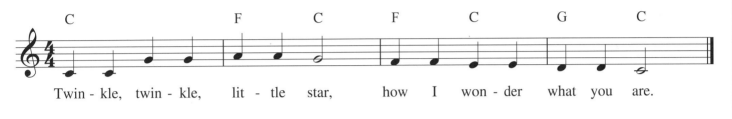

In the notated example above, notice that:

1. The chords are *above* each measure.

2. The melody line is written on a music staff using musical notes with different note values:

   ♩ = quarter note. A quarter note equals one beat in a measure.

   ♩ = half note. A half note equals two beats in a measure.

3. The lyrics are written below the staff and should line up with each note.

NOTATION EXAMPLE

One of my original songs is called "Maybe." It is more complex than an ABAB form, but for right now it serves as an example of something you can work up to! (If you'd like to hear to the song, it's available on my website at **www.allisonjamesmusic.com**, Apple Music, Spotify, YouTube, and all other digital streaming services.) On the next page is the first half of the lead sheet.

While the recording is in the key of A-flat Major, the lead sheet has been transposed to the key of C Major so that you can easily recognize some of the musical symbols and notes. Like "Twinkle, Twinkle" on the previous page, "Maybe" has a time signature of 4/4. Also like "Twinkle, Twinkle," the chords are *above* the staff, the lyrics are *below* the staff, and the melody notes are written *on* the staff.

Specific parts of the song are labeled so that you can see that it has a different form from your ABAB song. "Maybe" has a short **Introduction** (Intro), a **Verse**, a **Pre-Chorus**, and a **Chorus**. (A *Pre-Chorus* is a section of a song that directly precedes the Chorus and is repeated just like the Chorus—same melody, same lyrics. In a way, it acts as a lead up to the Chorus, preparing the listener for more of a climax when the Chorus finally occurs.)

This song brought unexpected tears to the eyes of the people I first played it for. See if you can feel the emotion it evokes. It also follows a lot of the suggestions we've learned thus far: the melody matches the mood of the lyrics, the song has a catchy hook, and the notes of the melody in the Chorus are higher than the notes of the melody in the Verse.

Listen to (and/or play) "Maybe" and come up with your own analysis of the song.

MAYBE

Music & Lyrics by Allison James

It's now your turn to notate.

NOTATION PRACTICE

Here is a chord chart for one verse and one chorus of "This Old Man":

$\frac{4}{4}$ | C C C C | C C C C | F F F F | G7 G7 G7 G7 |

Lyrics: This old man, ____ he played one, ____ He played knick-knack on his thumb with a

| C C C C | C C C C | G7 G7 G7 G7 | C C C C ‖

knick-knack paddy-whack, give the dog a bone, _ This old man came roll - ing home. ___

NOTE: Seventh chords, such as the G7 above,
are explained in the Additional Chords section on page 15.

Get better acquainted with "This Old Man."
Sing it through once or twice, as you play the chords on the guitar.

As a reminder, here are the chords on a guitar:

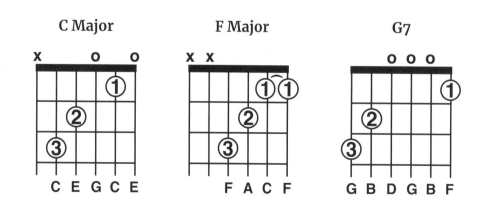

5A. Play the melody of "This Old Man."

The first step to notating melody is to play the melody line. Here's how to do it:

1. Play the first chord, so you start in the correct key.

2. Now hum or sing the first note of the song.

3. Find the matching note on the guitar. Use the fretboard below for reference to the notes.

4. By trial and error, continue adding notes of the melody as you find them on the guitar.

Continue this process until you can play the entire melody of the song.

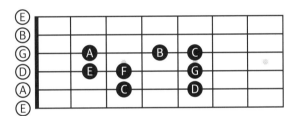

Your Turn

Following the steps above, use your ear to guide you through the melody line of "This Old Man."

Play the first verse and first chorus as shown in the example.

Sing along!

5B. Notate the melody of "This Old Man."

Now that you can play the melody, transfer what you played to the treble staff.

Use the following note values:

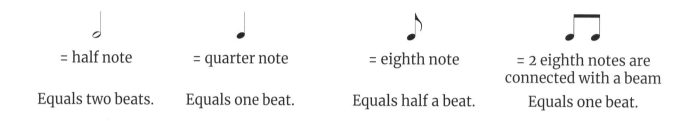

= half note	= quarter note	= eighth note	= 2 eighth notes are connected with a beam
Equals two beats.	Equals one beat.	Equals half a beat.	Equals one beat.

This song is in $\frac{4}{4}$ time, just like your song.

Your Turn

Write the chords for "This Old Man" into the chord chart
on the opposite page on the music staff provided.
[Hint: The chords are written on page 44.]

Write each note of the melody on the staff.
The first measure is done for you.
Play the melody for reference, as needed.

Write in the lyrics to match up with the melody.

Because "This Old Man" is in the key of C Major, these are your note options:

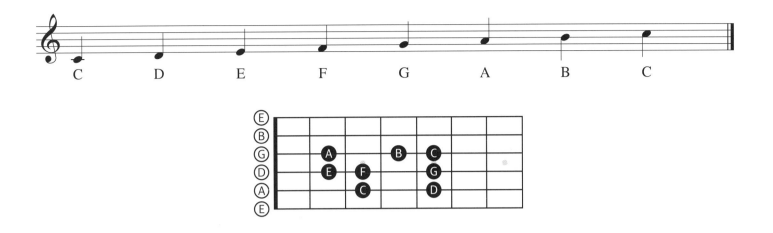

THIS OLD MAN

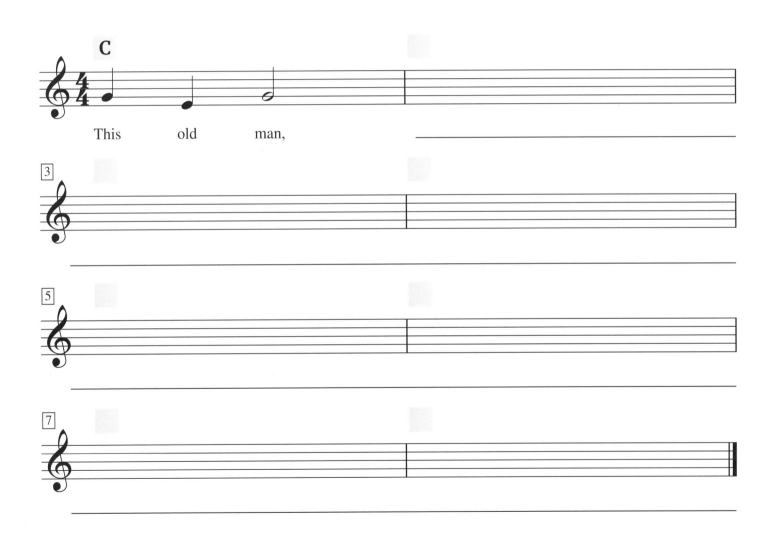

This   old   man,

[For reference, the completed notation is on page 53. Check that you've notated it correctly.]

NOTATING YOUR MELODY

5C. Play the chords.

Your Turn

Turn back to your original chord chart on page 37,
and play the chords in your song as you sing the melody.

5D. Play the melody.

Pick out the melody to your song on the guitar. Use the same process you used for "This Old Man":

1. Play the first chord, so you start in the correct key.
2. Hum or sing the first note of your song.
3. Find the matching note on the guitar.
4. By trial and error, add the notes of the melody as you find them on the guitar.

Continue this process until you can play the entire melody of your song.

Remember, your song has 2 sections of melody: one for the verse and one for the chorus.

2 sections of melody:
1 from the Verse (A section)
1 from the Chorus (B section)

Begin with the melody for the verse. Then add the melody for the chorus.

Your Turn

Find and play the melody of your song on the guitar.

5E. Notate your melody.

Now that you can play your melody, transfer what you have played to a treble staff. On the next couple pages, TWO charts are provided for you, the second in case you want a fresh sheet to revise or rewrite any parts of the song.

The first 4 staves will be for the VERSES; the second 4 staves will be for the CHORUS.

Since your melodies repeat, we will be using the repeat sign:

The repeat sign signals to the performer that the song should be repeated.

The two lines under the staves are for the lyrics. The 1st verse will go on line 1 and the 2nd verse will go on line 2. Since the chorus lyrics repeat, only one lyric line is needed.

Note values you can use include:

𝅝   whole note (4 beats)   ♩ quarter note (1 beat)

𝅗𝅥   half note (2 beats)   ♪ eighth note (1/2 beat)

𝅗𝅥. dotted half note (3 beats)   𝅘𝅥𝅯 sixteenth note (1/4 beat)

Your Turn

Write the chords for your song into the chord chart
on the next page in the grey boxes above each measure.

THEN

Write each note of your melody on the staff.
Play the melody for reference, as needed.

THEN

Write in the lyrics to match up with the melody.
[Revise as needed.]

TITLE

Music & Lyrics by _____

Verse: 1. _____

2. _____

5

9

13

17

Chorus: _____

21

25

29

TITLE

Music & Lyrics by _____

Verse: 1. _____
       2. _____

5

9

13

17

Chorus: _____

21

25

29

Congratulations!

You have written (and notated) your first song.

SHARE YOUR SONG WITH US

We would love to hear your finished song. Record audio or video of your song
and share it with us! Tag us and share your song with the hashtag: #writeyourfirstsong

 Facebook – @songwritingworkbooks

 Instagram – @songwritingworkbooks

 Twitter – @songwritingwbks

[From page 46]

For your reference, here is the written notation for "This Old Man."

Also Available

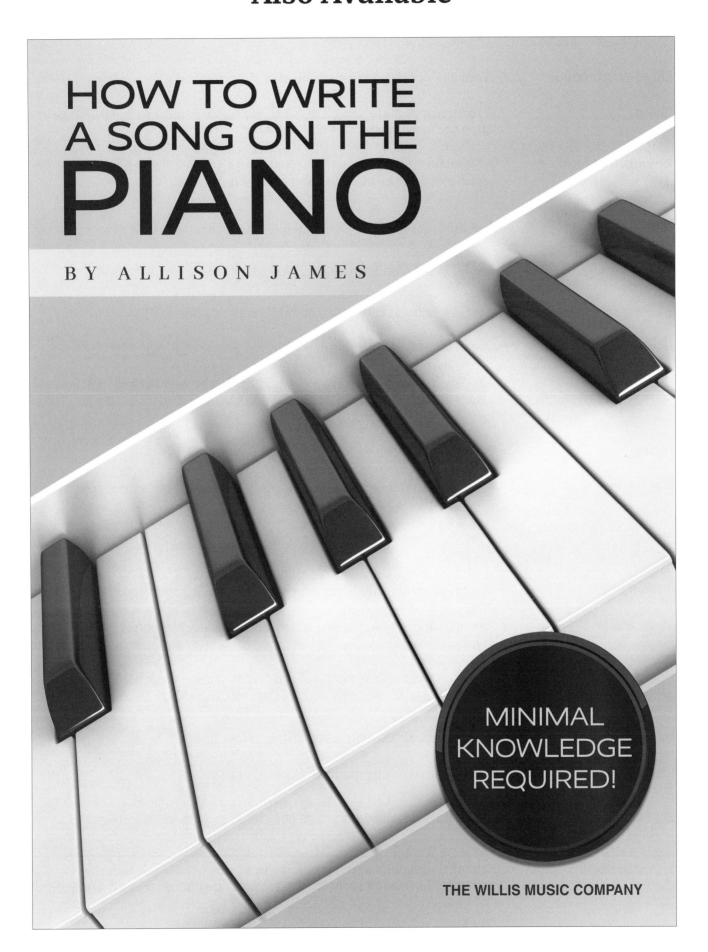

HOW TO WRITE
A SONG ON THE
PIANO

BY ALLISON JAMES

MINIMAL
KNOWLEDGE
REQUIRED!

THE WILLIS MUSIC COMPANY

HL 00293909

GLOSSARY

Chord A group of 3 or more notes played together.

Chord Chart or Lead Sheet A chart of chords for a song.

Chord Progression A sequence of chords played one after the other and then repeated.

Chorus A section or part of a song that is usually repeated after each verse. It is often the most memorable part of a song.

Diminished Chord A dissonant sounding chord. It consists of an interval of a minor 3rd on top of a minor 3rd. (A minor 3rd consists of 3 half steps).

Dotted Half Note A hollow musical note with a stem and a dot. It receives 3 beats.

Eighth Note A solid musical note with a stem and a flag. It receives half a beat.

Half Note A hollow musical note with a stem. It receives 2 beats.

Hook The main lyric idea and a catchy musical phrase of a song.

Key A tonal center of a song. The key signature is a group of sharps or flats placed at the beginning of a song (before the time signature). It establishes the tonality of the song or piece.

Lyrics The words to a melody in a song.

Major Chord A "happy" sounding chord. It consists of an interval of a minor 3rd on top of a major 3rd (4 half steps).

Melody A satisfying sequence of notes and rhythms. Lyrics are added to the melody in a song.

Minor Chord A "sad" sounding chord. An interval of a major 3rd on top of a minor 3rd.

Music Staff A set of 5 lines and 4 spaces. Each line and space represents a precise musical pitch.

Notation The act of writing down musical symbols (notes, rests, articulation, etc.) on a music staff.

Quarter Note A solid musical note with a stem. It receives one beat.

Rhythm The measured arrangement and flow of music.

Sixteenth Note A solid musical note with a stem and two flags. It receives a quarter of a beat.

Time Signature A numbered symbol at the beginning of a piece of music. It tells the performer how many beats are in each measure and what kind of note gets one beat.

Verse The section of a song that precedes the chorus. The verses are usually distinct and not repeated elsewhere in the song.

Whole Note A hollow musical note without a stem. It receives 4 beats.